i love me enough to let me go

johanna de vries

PRESS

Published 2021 by Artis Press, Calgary, Alberta
Copyright © 2021, Johanna De Vries.

All rights reserved. No part of this book may be used or reproduced, except for brief quotations in articles or reviews, without written permission from the author. For information, contact Artis Press: info@artispress.ca

ISBN: 978-1-9994721-4-6

Art, design, and editing by Elaine Ellis (elaineellis.ca)

To my husband Michael, Mom, Dad, and Kelly—
You continually inspire me.

To all the other poets out there—
I see your words like I see my own:
Release them.

cheers to you
you stopped listening to the sad songs
craving empathy to fill the emptiness
you fell asleep quickly tonight
you didn't count the ceiling dots
your smile broke through the concrete
your laugh sounded too loud in your ears
you didn't have the sound turned down too low
so drink up reasons that aren't tragic
this one is on you

i believe in pain
not in the same way i believe in God
but in the way
you say you are in pain
i believe you

i did the best i could
with the best i had
and now there is nothing left

it's not a case of the blues
it's a case of the greys
when all of my reds yellows purples greens
hues
have turned to shades
of what I used to be

your smile cannot stop me from spiralling
  but it sure makes it a lovely ride

i am desperate to feel
i scream for rain so i can be cold and wet and miserable
i beg for sunshine to coddle myself in warmth
i scrape my skin
i gouge my eyes
i cry in sharp pain
because if i don't bleed then i will be certain
the dead feel nothing
i want to throw myself at someone
in order to experience pure passion
i will kick in the doors and smash windows
please hate me
i want wrath and jealousy and sorrow
i want joy and love and horror
i want it all
the living must feel something

what doesn't kill is still in you
it may make you stronger
but in the end it may still kill you
even if you pray for longer

some would say i am too young to feel this sad
since when does depression have a due date
i think its about the pain inside
the numbness you feel
the losses you have faced
a crushed soul can't wait for adulthood
sadness doesn't have a monopoly on years
for the brightest years of my life
i sure can bring the darkness

what if the devil spoke into your ear
and the words he said
were your own worst fears
if he could see into your mind
if he could see into your heart
if he could see into all the things you said
just to keep yourself apart
from the masses and the friends and the loved
ones so dear
what would you do if the demons filled your ears

once in awhile
i place my hand on my chest
i lift it up and down with every breath
i lick my lips
i wiggle my toes
i unclench my jaw
and i blink
everything works
nothing is broken
i make sure i'm still here
even when i hope i'm not

if time is sand
then so are you
both have slipped through my fingers
and my skin has never been this dry

i picture a world without my anxiety
i dream of what i'd find
i imagine it's a galaxy full of words
beyond those that circle the cosmos of my mind

you made your love look like a gun
when you said i'm sorry
and pointed it at me

maybe there's a bigger purpose
maybe there's a better plan
i feel the weight of the planet beneath me
i am not strong enough to hold it up
not brave enough to even stand

maybe there's a God to save me
maybe there's a love out there
i am lost to make a move towards it
i hear echoes in the forest that surrounds me
of how when or where

my best chance is he'll come searching
maybe love will find me after all
maybe i'll lift my head up just enough
i'll see it coming
i'll hear it call
and i will answer

i heard that your voice is in the wind
so i let my hair blow just to let you in
i waited on that cliff and cried out your name
but i couldn't hear you answer me with the same
just an echo of my own pain

she smiled with ease
but then again
she cried so easily as well
how would you know

i just want to go back to bed
but when i wake up it won't be better
i'll still have your song in my head
i'll still be clutching your letter

if there is one thing i've learned in this life
it's that going through the motions
never got anyone to their destination

i don't know her face
but i do know her name
she is a stranger to me in the most familiar way
she holds burdens and secrets from a world i once
knew
she clutches deep at buried scars
and i can feel the sting
she is hiding deep within a dark place
she is the past i push through
she is the me that threatens to run
she is the hurt that doesn't want to heal
we are not one any more
i must throw her to the ground and wipe
both our tears from our cheeks
i will crush her soul
to save my own
goodbye

i'd rather be in the dark woods
than the city at night
the city has too many humans in it
i'm safer here

this pain will pass but until then you must be strong/ you must believe that you are more than how you feel right now/ you must have faith that there will indeed be more than right now/

        YOU MUST

        YOU MUST

        YOU MUST

if i could make the fire stop
that flares beneath my bones
if I could silence all the screams
that rise up in my throat
if i could catch the tidal wave
before it brings me to my knees
but if it all went to you instead
i'd gladly suffer endlessly

i rebuilt this shattered me you broke of me
piece by piece
as the glass sliced my hand
it was worth it
for this healed reflection

so i caught myself smiling today
it's been awhile
the realization
only made me smile more

my body is a battleground
my soul is a gladiator
i am armed for war

i knew i was going to be fine
the moment i stubbed my toe
i swore loud and clear
i understood
i can feel
i can feel again
i am real
i am real again

i will not seek my own refuge of relief
i will repress my desire to fade
i will slog through murky waters of pain
i will be licked by flames of sacrifice
i will exit upon divinity's will
i will not take this into my own hands again
i will choose to live

we are the lonely hearts
the torn a parts
the fresh starts

her heart didn't live on her sleeve
but in the base of her hand
and through each heartbreak
her fingers got a little more scarred
they aged with her
soon there were lines upon lines
and though she was not young any longer
she was still brave enough
to raise her hands heaven bound
fingers outstretched

a diary of mine reads
i got up today
well
i think
i guess i'll get up tomorrow too

heat rises
so will i

you deserve to do the things
that make you feel alive
after spending so much time
wishing you were dead

i love me enough
to let me go

lover

i asked her
do you remember
the boys that broke our hearts
i answered her
neither do i

loving you and losing you is
both a tsunami and a wildfire/
storms that brought change/
it is embers running through my veins/
it is seeing you in every sunrise and sunset/
it is knowing i will see you again, yet/
it is letting you go with no regret

do you remember how once we were
young and pretentious
driving through small town streets
simply looking for a place to park
so i could run my fingers through dark hair
and you could kiss me back
and we would talk and talk and talk for hours
do you remember us
loud and ridiculous
playing video games and yelling at television screens
laughing like nothing ever mattered
still there was nothing more important to us
do you remember you and me
simple and frivolous
walking everywhere there was
any excuse to link fingers
my how far those days seem now
when captioned by remember

our choices
make us
break us
forsake us
so what does it mean
if my choice has always been you

we meet up to talk
sipping coffee
and reminiscing about old days
you say to me
do you recall when we were happy and in love
i say
only in that order

there comes a point where he begins to fade/
his laugh, his smile, the way he said your name/
even some of the memories lose their color/ but
the hole he left never really disappears/ it will
throb a little more when someone says his name
or he looks your way/ when you realize how
empty his eyes are without the shine you used
to know/ with the realization he isn't beside you
anymore, holding you/ it will hurt when you
begin to wonder whether he cared about you at
all/ it doesn't make sense how this could possibly
happen and you attempt to reason it/ but you
can't/ there is no one left to blame – not even the
world/ you desperately grasp for the moments
as they slide from the front of your mind, not
because you want them to stay because you really
don't/ the hole should be closed and you should
move on/ except… you need those memories/
because with them, without every single pain and
ache and tear, you get to hold on to the goodness
a little longer/ the way it was will stay clutched
in your hand even when its blades dig into your

palm and leave scars/ if you let go of even the
tiniest drop of blood, he might just leave for
good/ and the fear grips you as you wonder what
your life would be without even his shadow in it/
so you don't sleep and you don't move, paralyzed
by that fear/ and despite your best efforts, he will
keep fading/ each time he does, you will miss him
a little more and hurt a little more and dream of
better days/ that is essentially heartbreak/
that is when you know you have truly loved

and when i say
i love you
i say it with lips made from roses
and thorns biting into my gums

i dreamed a little view of you
your head on my pillow
your hair in your eyes
i dreamed of your warm skin
the birthmark you hate
your crooked silly grin
i dreamed that you would stay
in this bed forever
and we could make stories
we could write songs
before we would fall asleep all over again
i dreamed a perfect view of you
and then i woke up

silence is golden
the tongue is silver
is this moment bronze
when we touch each other

i'm going to ask you to excuse the potholes
when you're running through my mind
you see they haven't all been filled yet
and they used to be quite deep

please excuse the pain
you might see in my eyes
you have a tendency to look through me
and I can't blink it away

please excuse those scars too
when you're examining my heart
they might make it slippery
and I don't want you to drop it

yes when you see my history
written all over my soul
remember that my past is how i got to you
and handle it with care

somehow we will fall in love
but you'll never touch the ground

tell me how you got in so fast
placed your hands against my protests
lowered my guarded fists
and opened my chest
to examine my heart
with surgical precision
locking the door behind you

like thunder you came
crashing in on my windows
pelting me with rain to kiss me under
the lightning flashed
in the brilliance you stood
for a moment
for a second
the storm that transformed my life

you are the smell of a leather couch
cool and comforting
you are the soft stroke of a rugged tree
its knots catching my fingers on the way down
as i dare to trail down to your roots
and see where you begin
you are my comfortable home
you are the wild outside

i remember how you kissed me
your mouth tasting like whiskey
and i got a little tipsy
on you

your heart
the way it fits in my hands
i could crush into tiny nevermore bits
and you would drop to the ground to catch the
pieces
and as each would fall further from okay
you would understand heartbreak
you see your heart is a vulnerable thing
and yet you have given it to me
not stolen
not taken
but left in my hands
your heart
it's a treasure to keep
it's a pleasure to keep

there are days i get so lost in my thoughts
i think that i'm in yours

i fall in love with people who talk to me at 2 am
it is then they are most honest
and most human
i fall in love with those who receive a piece of
good news
and their faces light up like the sun
my heart brightens with them
i fall in love with humans
who walk without headphones
and speak to bussing strangers
i guess i fall in love with folks
who seem to comprehend
the important moments
i most often forget

i wrote you a poem
then i crumpled it up
these words were not enough
they didn't convey calloused hands
warm laughter
soft lips
matching tea mugs
cold sheets
quick retorts
dances by the sink
the i dos
i wills
i ams

we are the bruised and the broken
we are the lost and the chosen
we are the weak and the weary
we are the ones who see clearly
we are the dark and depraved
we are the loved and the saved
we are the flawed and the failed
we are ones who will prevail

last night
i looked up at the stars
and sighed
i'm never going to remember any of this
"don't worry"
my heart whispered back
"i will"

Johanna De Vries is a Canadian poet, emerging playwright, and lover of the English language. She enjoys telling stories through spoken word poetry and has shared her work in venues all over Alberta.

Johanna currently resides in Calgary, Alberta, with her husband Michael and her cat Rogue. I Love Me Enough to Let Me Go is her debut collection of poetry. You can connect with Johanna on Facebook or Instagram @jdegiebs.

Made in the USA
Columbia, SC
26 February 2021